# Jesus on trial

Story by Penny Frank

Illustrated by John Haysom

THE LION
STORY BIBLE

47

TRING · BATAVIA · SYDNEY

The Bible tells us how God sent his Son Jesus to show us what God is like and how we can belong to God's kingdom.

This story tells how Jesus was arrested. He was accused of crimes he never committed, and killed by being fixed with nails onto a cross of wood.

You can find this story — the story of the first Good Friday — in your own Bible, near the end of all four Gospels — Matthew, Mark, Luke and John.

Copyright © 1987 Lion Publishing

Published by
**Lion Publishing plc**
Icknield Way, Tring, Herts, England
ISBN 0 85648 772 4
**Lion Publishing Corporation**
1705 Hubbard Avenue, Batavia,
Illinois 60510, USA
ISBN 0 85648 772 4
**Albatross Books Pty Ltd**
PO Box 320, Sutherland, NSW 2232, Australia
ISBN 0 86760 557 X

First edition 1987
Reprinted 1987

Printed and bound in Hong Kong

**British Library Cataloguing in Publication Data**

Frank, Penny
Jesus on trial.—(The Lion Story Bible;
47)
1. Jesus Christ—Passion—Juvenile
literature 2. Jesus Christ—Crucifixion—
Juvenile literature
I. Title    II. Haysom, John
232.9'6    BT431
ISBN 0-85648-772-4

**Library of Congress Cataloging in Publication Data**

Frank, Penny.
Jesus on trial.
(The Lion Story Bible; 47)
1. Jesus .Christ—Trial—Juvenile
literature. 2. Bible stories, English—
N.T. Gospels. [1. Jesus Christ—Passion.
2. Bible stories—N.T.]
I. Haysom, John, ill. II. Title. III.
Series: Frank, Penny. Lion Story Bible;
47.
BT440.F73 1987    232.9'62    86-4347
ISBN 0-85648-772-4

Jesus and the disciples were in
Jerusalem. They had eaten the special
Passover meal together. Then they had
walked slowly out of the city, up the
steep road to the orchard of olive-trees,
called the Garden of Gethsemane.

'Stay here,' Jesus said, 'while I talk to God my Father. Pray for me. This is the most difficult hour of my life.'

Jesus went and knelt down on the ground.

'Please save me from all this pain and agony,' he called out to God. 'How can I bear it? But if I must die, so that you can bring people into your kingdom, I am willing to die.'

When he came back to the disciples, they were fast asleep. Jesus woke them up.

'Couldn't you stay awake, just for me?' he asked.

'Look,' Jesus said. 'There are people coming to arrest me.'

They could see the soldiers coming through the trees, with lights and swords.

The disciples began to feel afraid.

Then they saw that the man leading the soldiers was one of the disciples — their friend Judas. But he did not look at them.

The priests had paid Judas a lot of money to help them catch Jesus. Judas went up to Jesus and kissed him, to show the soldiers which man to arrest.

The crowd of soldiers gathered around Jesus, with swords drawn.

'You don't need those swords,' Jesus said. 'Didn't you notice me in the temple today? Why didn't you arrest me then?'

The disciples were so afraid that they all ran away into the darkness of the garden.

When the soldiers had taken Jesus away, the disciples went back to the little room where they had eaten supper together. Only Simon Peter turned back. He crept along behind the soldiers, to see where they took Jesus.

Jesus was taken to the house of the chief priest. The priests had decided to arrest and question Jesus at night. In the daytime he was always with crowds of people.

Jesus had not done anything wrong, so
the priests had to pay people to come
and tell lies about him.

Simon Peter followed the soldiers. But when they took Jesus away to question him, Simon Peter waited outside with some of the servants. He came closer to the fire, to keep warm.

Simon Peter heard the chief priest say to Jesus, 'Is it true that you are God's Son — the one he promised to send?'

'I am,' Jesus answered.

'Now we've heard your lies for ourselves,' they shouted. 'We will have you killed, because you have pretended to be God's Son.'

Outside in the dark, a servant girl came up to the fire and looked at Simon Peter. The firelight flickered on his face as he held his hands close to the burning logs.

'Aren't you one of the disciples of Jesus?' she said.

Simon Peter was frightened.

'No, of course I'm not,' he said quickly. 'I've never even met him.' Three times he said the same thing.

14

Then it was dawn, and a cock crowed. As Jesus was led away, he looked at Simon Peter.

'I promised tonight that I would always be his friend,' Simon Peter thought. 'And now I've said I don't even know him.'

Then Simon Peter ran away, crying.

The soldiers then took Jesus to Pilate, the Emperor's ruler in Jerusalem.

'Are you trying to become a king?' Pilate asked Jesus. The Emperor would not like that!

'My kingdom does not belong to this world,' Jesus said. 'You say that I am a king. But I came into this world only to tell people about God's truth.'

'Well then, I don't know what all this trouble is about,' said Pilate. He went outside to the priests.

'I can't find anything this man has done wrong,' said Pilate.

'He pretends to be God's Son. By our law he must die,' shouted the priests.

18

'What has he done?' asked Pilate. But
they just shouted, 'Crucify him! Crucify
him!'

Pilate was tired of arguing. He was
afraid there would be a riot. The
Emperor would not like that. So he
agreed that Jesus should be crucified.

20

The priests were very pleased. They were going to get rid of Jesus at last.

All the people who loved Jesus watched sadly, as he carried the wooden cross up the hill, out of the city. They had wanted Jesus to be their king.

Jesus knew he was finishing the work God had given him to do.

Jesus looked down from the cross. He saw his disciples and his mother, Mary.

He knew that when he died they would be very sad.

So he said to John, one of his special friends, 'Look after my mother for me, John, as if you were her son.'

'Forgive these people, Father,' he said to God. 'They don't know what they are doing.'

Then Jesus died.

'He really was the Son of God,' said one of the soldiers standing guard.

The disciples were very sad. They thought that everything was over. They would never see Jesus again. But they were wrong!

**The Lion Story Bible** is made up of 52 individual stories for young readers, building up an understanding of the Bible as one story — God's story — a story for all time and all people.

The New Testament section (numbers 31–52) covers the life and teaching of God's Son, Jesus. The stories are about the people he met, what he did and what he said. Almost all we know about the life of Jesus is recorded in the four Gospels — Matthew, Mark, Luke and John. The word gospel means 'good news'.

The last four stories in this section are about the first Christians, who started to tell others the 'good news', as Jesus had commanded them — a story which continues today all over the world.

All four New Testament Gospels record the arrest, trial and death of Jesus: Matthew, chapters 26–27; Mark, chapters 14–15; Luke, chapters 22–23; John, chapters 18–19.

Jesus knew, long before he reached Jerusalem, that he would be arrested and killed. At least three times he had tried to warn his disciples, but they did not understand.

It is clear from all the accounts that the charges brought against him were false. Governor Pilate could not find him guilty, and pronounced the sentence only because of a threatened revolt.

'I am the good shepherd,' Jesus said. 'I lay down my life for the sheep. No one takes it from me. I lay it down of my own accord.'

We were the ones who deserved that sentence, for all the wrong we have done. Jesus paid the penalty for us, once and for all.

The next book in the series, number 48: *The first Easter*, tells the story of the happiest day ever.